Butterfly, Flea, Beetle, and Bee

Insect:
an animal that has six legs and a body divided in three parts

Butterfly, Flea, Beetle, and Bee

What Is an Insect?

by Brian P. Cleary

illustrations by Martin Goneau

M Millbrook Press • Minneapolis

An **insect** is an animal that always has six legs.

hatches from egg

Most have two antennas, and they all are born from eggs.

The body of an **insect** is divided in three parts:

an abdomen,

a thorax,

and a head
(for **insect** smarts).

Unlike you and me, they have no backbone and no lungs.

But they have something near their mouths called palps they use like tongues!

An outer exoskeleton,
a sturdy type of shell,

supports an **insect's** muscles while protecting it as well.

Insects breathe through openings they have along each side,

SPIRACLES

allowing them to take in air
at rest or while in stride.

So, just what are the names of those that carry all these features?

Once you've finished this, you'll know a host of different creatures!

Yellow jackets,

fireflies,

the termite,

and mosquito.

A giant hissing cockroach
half as long as a burrito!

Some **insects** like to creak or croon.
One even seems to speak!

Some chirp, and some will buzz or hum,
while others kind of squeak.

They grow by metamorphosis, often in four stages:

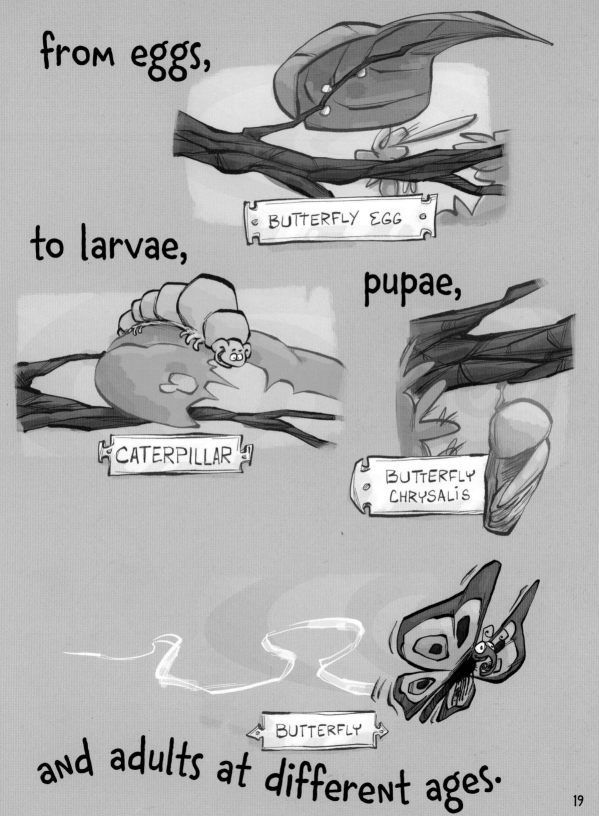

from eggs,

BUTTERFLY EGG

to larvae,

pupae,

CATERPILLAR

BUTTERFLY
CHRYSALIS

BUTTERFLY

and adults at different ages.

19

Three-part metamorphosis is known as incomplete.

EGG

NYMPH

ADULT

Crickets, for example,
grow in three steps as they eat.

Flies have just one pair of wings, but most **insects** have two,

connecting to the thorax
where you'll find their six legs too.

Insects live in trees and water,

dirt and— YUCK!— your hair!

Some can live in socks
and shirts and even underwear!

Take Walking sticks
and silverfish
and grasshoppers and lice

and big goliath beetles that can
weigh as much as mice.

All of these are **insects**, like the common clothing moth

whose larvae (not the moth itself) will eat through woolen cloth!

I sure don't mean to "bug" you,
but make certain that you look

at all the **insect** info in the last part of this book!

So, what is an **insect**? Do you know?

An animal is an insect if . . .
- it has six legs;
- its body is divided in three parts: the head, thorax, and abdomen;
- it does not have a backbone (it's an invertebrate).

In addition, all insects . . .

- have a hard outer covering called an exoskeleton;
- breathe air through openings called spiracles along the thorax;
- lay eggs;
- grow through a process called metamorphosis. Babies are called larvas or nymphs. They shed their skin and change form in stages to become adults.

And most insects . . .

- have one pair of antennas;
- have two pairs of wings. The wings and legs are attached to the thorax.

INSECTS ONLY

Find activities, games, and more at
www.brianpcleary.com

ABOUT THE AUTHOR & THE ILLUSTRATOR

BRIAN P. CLEARY is the author of the Words Are
CATegorical®, Math Is CATegorical®, Adventures
in Memory™, Sounds Like Reading®, and Food Is
CATegorical™ series, as well as several picture books
and poetry books. He lives in Cleveland, Ohio.

MARTIN GONEAU is the illustrator of the Food Is
CATegorical™ series. He lives in Trois-Rivières, Québec.

LERNER 🄴 SOURCE™

Expand learning beyond this printed book.
Download free, complementary educational
resources for this book from our website,
www.lernerresource.com.

Text copyright © 2013 by Brian P. Cleary
Illustrations copyright © 2013 by Lerner Publishing Group, Inc.

Millbrook Press
A division of Lerner Publishing Group, Inc.
241 First Avenue North
Minneapolis, MN 55401 U.S.A.

Website address: www.lernerbooks.com

Dragonfly Wing Background: © Reinhold Leitner/Shutterstock.com.

Main body text set in Chauncy Decaf Medium 35/44. Typeface provided by the Chank Company.

Library of Congress Cataloging-in-Publication Data

Cleary, Brian P., 1959–
    Butterfly, flea, beetle, and bee : what is an insect? / by Brian P. Cleary ; illustrated by Martin Goneau.
        p.   cm. — (Animal groups are CATegorical)
    ISBN 978-0-7613-6208-1 (lib. bdg. : alk. paper)
    1. Insects—Juvenile literature. I. Goneau, Martin, ill. II. Title.
QL467.2.C654   2013
595.7—dc23   2011044871

Manufactured in the United States of America
1 – DP – 7/15/2012